IT'S TIME TO EAT SNACK MIX

It's Time to Eat SNACK MIX

Walter the Educator

Silent King Books
A WhichHead Entertainment Imprint

Copyright © 2024 by Walter the Educator

All rights reserved. No part of this book may be reproduced in any manner whatsoever without written per- mission except in the case of brief quotations embodied in critical articles and reviews.

First Printing, 2024

Disclaimer

This book is a literary work; the story is not about specific persons, locations, situations, and/or circumstances unless mentioned in a historical context. Any resemblance to real persons, locations, situations, and/or circumstances is coincidental. This book is for entertainment and informational purposes only. The author and publisher offer this information without warranties expressed or implied. No matter the grounds, neither the author nor the publisher will be accountable for any losses, injuries, or other damages caused by the reader's use of this book. The use of this book acknowledges an understanding and acceptance of this disclaimer.

It's Time to Eat SNACK MIX is a collectible early learning book by Walter the Educator suitable for all ages belonging to Walter the Educator's Time to Eat Book Series. Collect more books at WaltertheEducator.com

USE THE EXTRA SPACE TO TAKE NOTES AND DOCUMENT YOUR MEMORIES

SNACK MIX

It's time to munch, it's time to crunch,

It's Time to Eat

Snack Mix

Snack mix is ready, our favorite lunch!

A handful here, a handful there,

Delicious treasures everywhere!

Crunchy pretzels, salty and round,

Cheesy bites that make a sound.

Sweet chocolate chips, oh what a treat,

Snack mix is the best to eat!

Tiny crackers, shapes galore,

.

Each bite leaves you wanting more.

Golden raisins, soft and sweet,

Every piece is fun to meet!

Mix them up, swirl them around,

Snack mix magic can be found.

Take a nibble, big or small,

Snack mix fun is loved by all!

It's Time to Eat

Snack Mix

Share with friends or keep your own,

Snack time joy is brightly shown.

One by one, or by the bunch,

Perfect for a morning crunch!

Scoop it up or pour it out,

Snack mix makes us sing and shout.

Little fingers grab with care,

Yummy goodness everywhere!

A bite of this, a bite of that,

Snack mix is where the flavors chat.

Salty, sweet, and oh so nice,

Every handful, paradise!

So grab a bag or fill your bowl,

Snack mix warms your hungry soul.

When snack time calls, we're on the way,

It's Time to Eat

Snack Mix

Snack mix makes the perfect day!

One last bite, and then we're done,

Snack mix time is always fun!

Until next time, we'll think of you,

Our tasty mix, a dream come true!

Let's give a cheer, hooray for snack!

A tasty mix we always pack.

It's Time to Eat

Snack
Mix

For school, for trips, or at the park,

Snack mix brightens every spark!

ABOUT THE CREATOR

Walter the Educator is one of the pseudonyms for Walter Anderson. Formally educated in Chemistry, Business, and Education, he is an educator, an author, a diverse entrepreneur, and he is the son of a disabled war veteran. "Walter the Educator" shares his time between educating and creating. He holds interests and owns several creative projects that entertain, enlighten, enhance, and educate, hoping to inspire and motivate you. Follow, find new works, and stay up to date with Walter the Educator™

at WaltertheEducator.com

www.ingramcontent.com/pod-product-compliance
Lightning Source LLC
LaVergne TN
LVHW052015060526
838201LV00059B/4038